Your first 100 words in RUSSIAN

Beginner's Quick & Easy Guide to Demystifying Russian Script

Series concept
Jane Wightwick

Illustrations
Mahmoud Gaafar

Russian edition
Helena Chick

Давид

Давид

PASSPORT BOOKS
NTC/Contemporary Publishing Group

Other titles in this series:

Your First 100 Words in Arabic
Your First 100 Words in Chinese
Your First 100 Words in Japanese

Cover design by Nick Panos

Published by Passport Books
A division of NTC/Contemporary Publishing Group, Inc.
4255 West Touhy Avenue, Lincolnwood (Chicago), Illinois 60712-1975 U.S.A.
Copyright © 1999 by Gaafar & Wightwick
Printed in the United States of America
International Standard Book Number: 0-8442-2398-0

99 00 01 02 03 04 VL 19 18 17 16 15 14 13 12 11 10 9 8 7 6 5 4 3 2 1

◎ CONTENTS

INTRODUCTION

In this activity book you'll find 100 key words for you to learn to read in Russian. All of the activities are designed specifically for reading non-Latin script languages. Many of the activities are inspired by the kind of games used to teach children to read their own language: flashcards, matching games, memory games, joining exercises, etc. This is not only a more effective method of learning to read a new script, but also much more fun.

We've included a **Scriptbreaker** to get you started. This is a friendly introduction to the Russian script that will give you tips on how to remember the letters.

Then you can move on to the 8 **Topics**. Each topic presents essential words in large type. There is also a pronunciation guide so you know how to say the words. These words are also featured in the tear-out **Flashcard** section at the back of the book. When you've mastered the words, you can go on to try out the activities and games for that topic.

There's also a **Round-up** section to review all your new words and the **Answers** to all the activities to check yourself.

Follow this 4-step plan for maximum success:

1 Have a look at the key topic words with their pictures. Then tear out the flashcards and shuffle them. Put them Russian side up. Try to remember what the word means and turn the card over to check with the English. When you can do this, cover the pronunciation and try to say the word and remember the meaning by looking at the Russian script only.

2 Put the cards English side up and try to say the Russian word. Try the cards again each day both ways around. (When you can remember a card for 7 days in a row, you can file it!)

3 Try out the activities and games for each topic. This will reinforce your recognition of the key words.

4 After you have covered all the topics, you can try the activities in the Round-up section to test your knowledge of all the Russian words in the book. You can also try shuffling all the flashcards together to see how many you can remember.

This flexible and fun way of reading your first words in Russian should give you a head start whether you're learning at home or in a group.

◎ SCRIPTBREAKER

The purpose of this Scriptbreaker is to introduce you to the Russian script and how it is formed. You should not try to memorize the alphabet at this stage, nor try to write the letters yourself. Instead, have a quick look through this section and then move on to the topics, glancing back if you want to work out the letters in a particular word. Remember, though, that recognizing the whole shape of the word in an unfamiliar script is just as important as knowing how it is made up. Using this method you will have a much more instinctive recall of vocabulary and will gain the confidence to expand your knowledge in other directions.

The Russian script – more properly called the Cyrillic script – is not nearly as difficult as it might seem at first glance. There are many letters that are the same as the English ones, there are capital letters, and, unlike English, words are usually spelled as they sound:

- Russian spelling and pronunciation are much more systematic than in English
- You will recognize some of the letters straight away, but beware of false friends!

◎ The alphabet

There are 32 letters in the Cyrillic alphabet. A good way of learning the alphabet is to take it in two stages.

Stage 1

The first stage consists of twenty relatively "easy" letters.

Six of these letters closely resemble their English equivalents. These are:

а *(a)*	е/ё *(ye/yo)*	К *(k)*
М *(m)*	О *(o or a)*	Т *(t)*

Five are misleading because they resemble English letters but are not equivalents:

В *(v)*	Н *(n)*	р *(r)*
С *(s)*	У *(oo)*	

We can now use these letters to make some words:

там *(tam)*	нос *(nos)*
рука *(rooka)*	утка *(ootka)*

The remaining nine letters are less familar shapes:

б *(b)*	Г *(g)*	Д *(d)*
З *(z)*	И *(ee)*	Й *(y)*
Л *(l)*	П *(p)*	ф *(f)*

We can use these letters to make some more words:

СТУЛ *(stool)*   СПИНА *(speena)*

ПЛИТА *(pleeta)*   ГДЕ *(gdye)*

- ✔ Russian has 32 letters
- ✔ Some letters are like their English equivalents
- ✔ Some letters look like their English equivalents, but are **false friends**

Stage 2

Stage two consists of the final 12 letters; all of these are again less familiar shapes.

The following six letters are individual letters in Russian, where in English a similar sound is made by putting two or more letters together:

Ж *(zh)*   Х *(kh)*   Ц *(ts)*

Ч *(ch)*   Ш *(sh)*   Щ *(shch)*

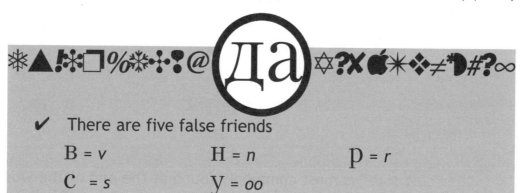

- ✔ There are five false friends

В = *v*   Н = *n*   Р = *r*

С = *s*   У = *oo*

Now look at these words:

ШКАФ *(shkaf)*   ШКОЛА *(shkola)*

ХОЛМ *(kholm)*   ЖИВОТ *(zheevot)*

The next four letters are all vowels:

Ы *(i)*   Э *(e)*

Ю *(yoo)*   Я *(ya)*

The final two letters, although part of the Cyrillic alphabet, can more easily be thought of as "signs" than as letters. Indeed, they are called the "hard sign" and the "soft sign." They do not really have a sound value, but rather affect the letters that precede or follow them.

Ъ *(hard sign)*   Ь *(soft sign)*

Now look at these words:

рыба *(riba)*   дверь *(dvyer')*
чистый *(cheestiy)*   туфля *(tooflya)*

Pronunciation tips

This activity has simplified some aspects of pronunciation in order to emphasize the basics. Don't worry at this stage about being precisely correct – the other letters in a word will help you to be understood.

Many Russian letters are pronounced in a similar way to their English equivalents, but here are a few which need special attention:

е and ё   although they are pronounced quite differently (*ye* and *yo*), these letters are considered to form a single letter of the Russian alphabet. In Russian books the two dots in ё are often omitted.

О   often pronounced as "*a.*" This happens when "*o*" is in an unstressed position in the word

Х   pronounced like the "*ch*" in the Yiddish "*chutzpah*".

Щ   pronounced like "*sh*" followed by "*ch*", as in "*pushchair*"

Ы   a tricky sound; try saying the "*ea*" as in "*tea*" and then, with the mouth in the same position, try saying "*oo*" as in "*boot*"

р   pronounced rolled at the front of the mouth

й   this letter occurs mainly after vowels, forming diphthongs, and is like the "*y*" in "*boy*"

ь   the "soft sign" is most commonly found at the end of the word, or is followed by a consonant. In these two cases it is not pronounced at all, but indicates that the preceding consonant is "soft" in sound. When the "soft sign" precedes a vowel, it is pronounced like "*y*" in "*yet*"

ъ   the "hard sign" does not occur often. It always precedes a vowel and is pronounced like "*y*" in "*yet;*" it also makes the preceding consonant "hard" in sound

This book also includes underscoring to show you which part of the word is stressed (pronounced with more emphasis). Remember, though, that the guidelines are only approximate and that you will find natural pronunciation sometimes deviates from these rules.

- ✔ Many Russian letters are pronounced in a similar way to English

- ✔ Russian spelling is much more straightforward than that of English

- ✔ You will often hear see "o" written, but hear it pronounced "a"

Summary of the Russian/Cyrillic alphabet

The table below shows all the Russian letters, both capitals and lower case. Hopefully, you will already recognize some of them, and as you move through the topics, they will become more familiar to you.

А	а	a	И	и	ee	С	с	s	Ъ	ъ	hard sign
Б	б	b	Й	й	y	Т	т	t	Ы	ы	i
В	в	v	К	к	k	У	у	oo	Ь	ь	soft sign
Г	г	g	Л	л	l	Ф	ф	f			
Д	д	d	М	м	m	Х	х	kh	Э	э	e
Е	е	ye	Н	н	n	Ц	ц	ts	Ю	ю	yoo
Ё	ё	yo	О	о	o	Ч	ч	chy	Я	я	ya
Ж	ж	zh	П	п	p	Ш	ш	sh			
З	з	z	Р	р	r	Щ	щ	shch			

8

① AROUND THE HOME

Look at the pictures of things you might find in a house.
Tear out the flashcards for this topic.
Follow steps 1 and 2 of the plan in the introduction.

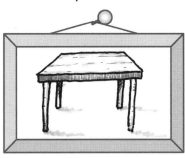

стол
stol

телевизор
*tele**vee**zar*

окно
*ak**no***

стул
stool

компьютер
*kam**pyoo**ter*

телефон
*tele**fon***

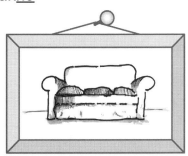

софа *so**fa***

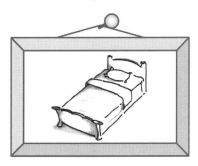

кровать *krav**at'***

холодильник
*khala**deel'**neek*

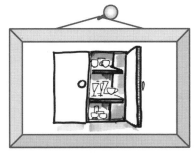

шкаф
shkaf

плита
*pl**ee**ta*

дверь
dvyer'

9

Match the pictures with the words, as in the example.

софа

кровать

окно

стол

телевизор

компьютер

телефон

стул

Now match the Russian household words to the English.

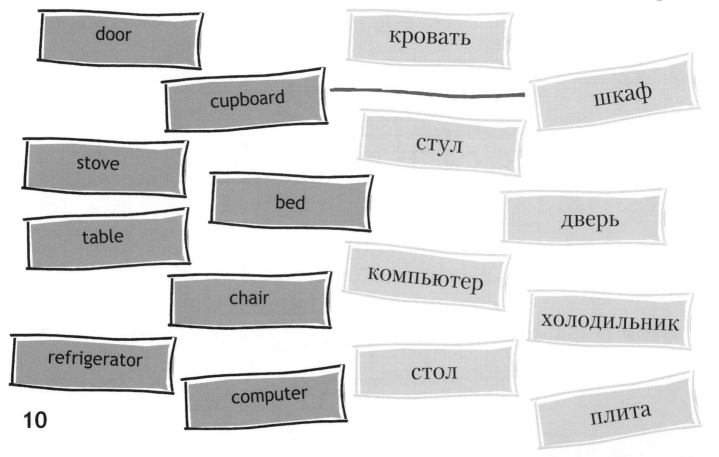

door

кровать

cupboard

шкаф

стул

stove

bed

дверь

table

компьютер

chair

холодильник

refrigerator

стол

computer

плита

Match the words and their pronunciation.

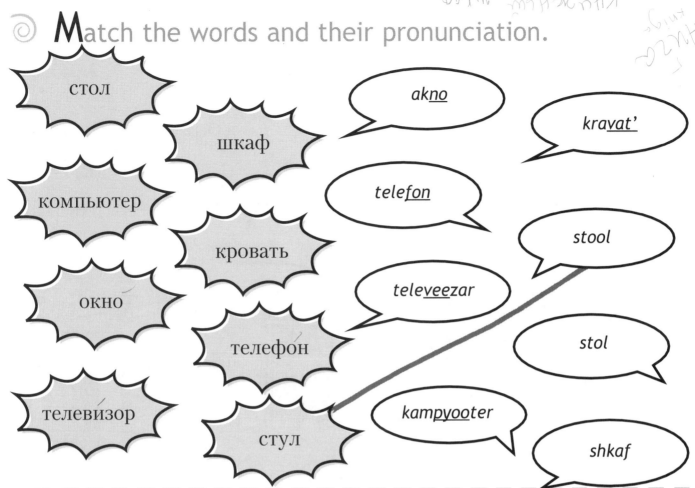

стол

шкаф

компьютер

кровать

окно

телефон

телевизор

стул

akno

kravat'

telefon

stool

televeezar

stol

kampyooter

shkaf

See if you can find these words in the word square.

The words can run left to right, or top to bottom:

плита

кровать

стул

стол

дверь

софа

П	Т	Д	Т	О	Л	С	П
Т	К	Р	О	В	А	Т	Ь
В	С	Л	Ь	П	У	У	В
Л	С	Т	О	Л	Ф	Л	О
Д	А	Д	В	Е	Р	Ь	С
Т	Ь	Т	О	Ь	Л	Х	О
П	Л	И	Т	А	Д	Н	Ф
К	И	О	В	А	П	Е	А

11

Decide where the household items should go. Then write the correct number in the picture, as in the example.

1. стол
2. стул
3. софа
4. телевизор
5. телефон
6. кровать
7. шкаф
8. плита
9. холодильник
10. компьютер
11. окно
12. дверь

Now see if you can fill in the household word at the bottom of the page by choosing the correct Russian.

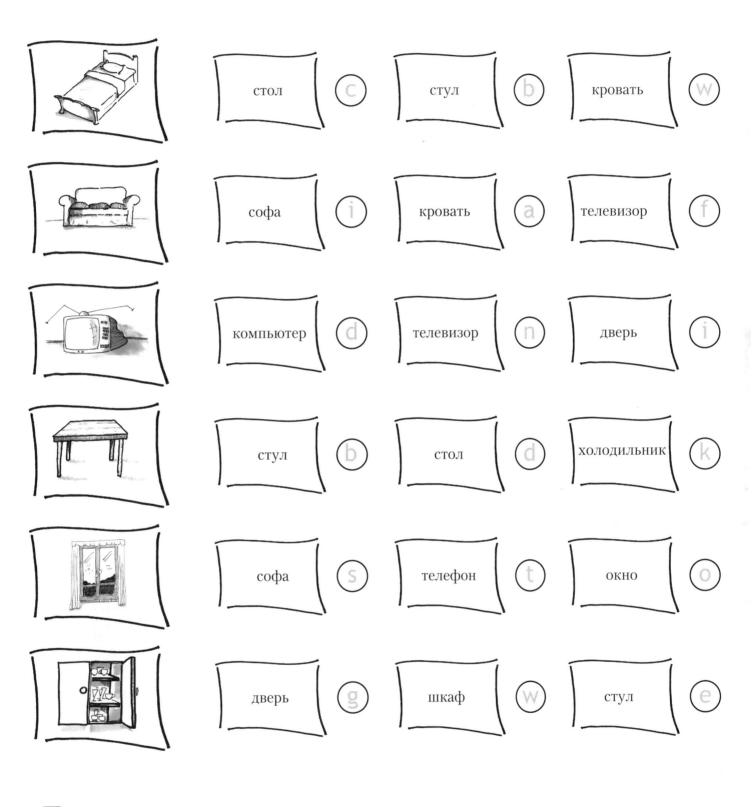

стол ⓒ	стул ⓑ	кровать ⓦ
софа ⓘ	кровать ⓐ	телевизор ⓕ
компьютер ⓓ	телевизор ⓝ	дверь ⓘ
стул ⓑ	стол ⓓ	холодильник ⓚ
софа ⓢ	телефон ⓣ	окно ⓞ
дверь ⓖ	шкаф ⓦ	стул ⓔ

English word: ⓦ ⓘ ⓝ ⓓ ⓞ ⓦ

② CLOTHES

Look at the pictures of different clothes.
Tear out the flashcards for this topic.
Follow steps 1 and 2 of the plan in the introduction.

ремень
remyen'

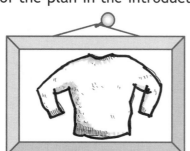

пуловер
poolover

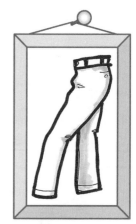

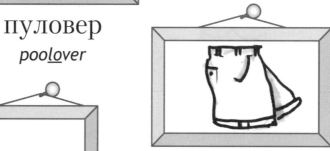

шорты
shorti

брюки
bryookee

носок
nasok

футболка
footbolka

пальто
pal'to

юбка
yoopka

платье
plat'e

шляпа *shlyapa*

туфля *tooflya*   рубашка *roobashka*

Match the Russian words and their pronunciation.

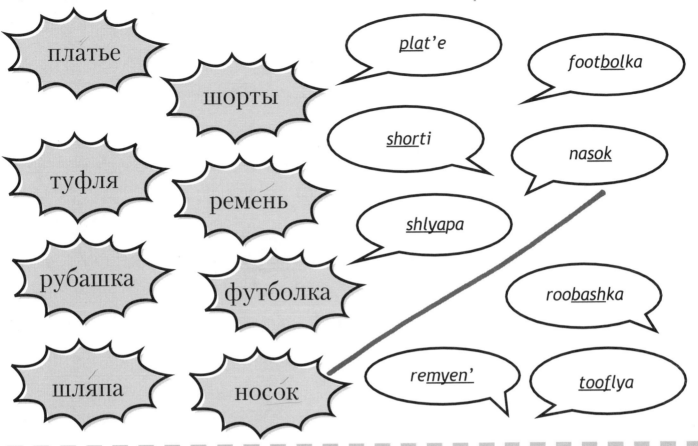

платье

шорты

plat'e

footbolka

shorti

nasok

туфля

ремень

shlyapa

рубашка

футболка

roobashka

шляпа

носок

remyen'

tooflya

See if you can find these clothes in the word square.

The words can run left to right, or top to bottom:

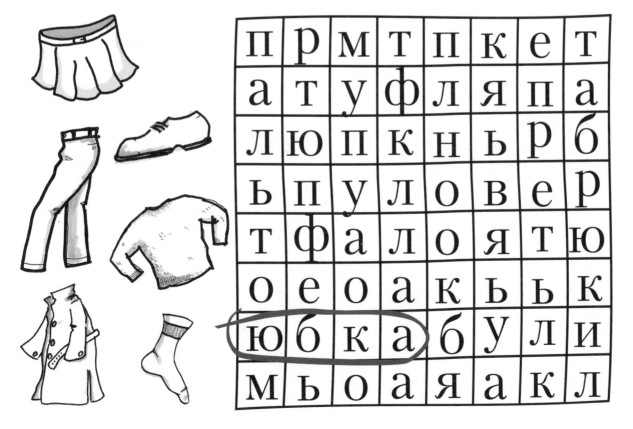

п	р	м	т	п	к	е	т
а	т	у	ф	л	я	п	а
л	ю	п	к	н	ь	р	б
ь	п	у	л	о	в	е	р
т	ф	а	л	о	я	т	ю
о	е	о	а	к	ь	ь	к
ю	б	к	а	б	у	л	и
м	ь	о	а	я	а	к	л

15

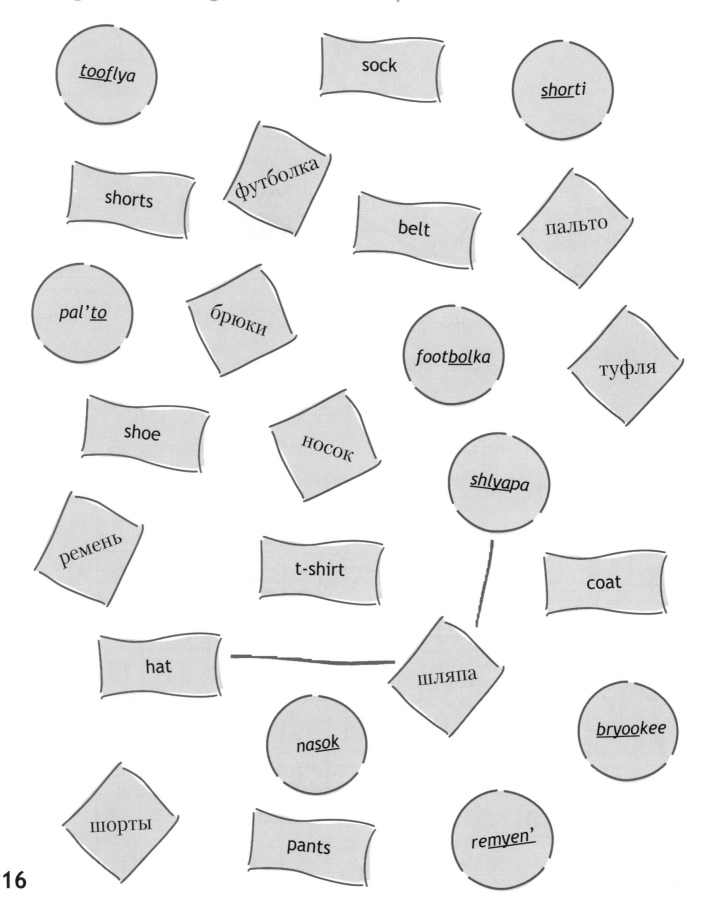

tooflya

sock

shorti

shorts

футболка

belt

пальто

pal'to

брюки

footbolka

туфля

shoe

носок

shlyapa

ремень

t-shirt

coat

hat

шляпа

bryookee

nasok

шорты

pants

remyen'

16

Candy is going on vacation. Count how many of each type of clothing she is packing in her suitcase.

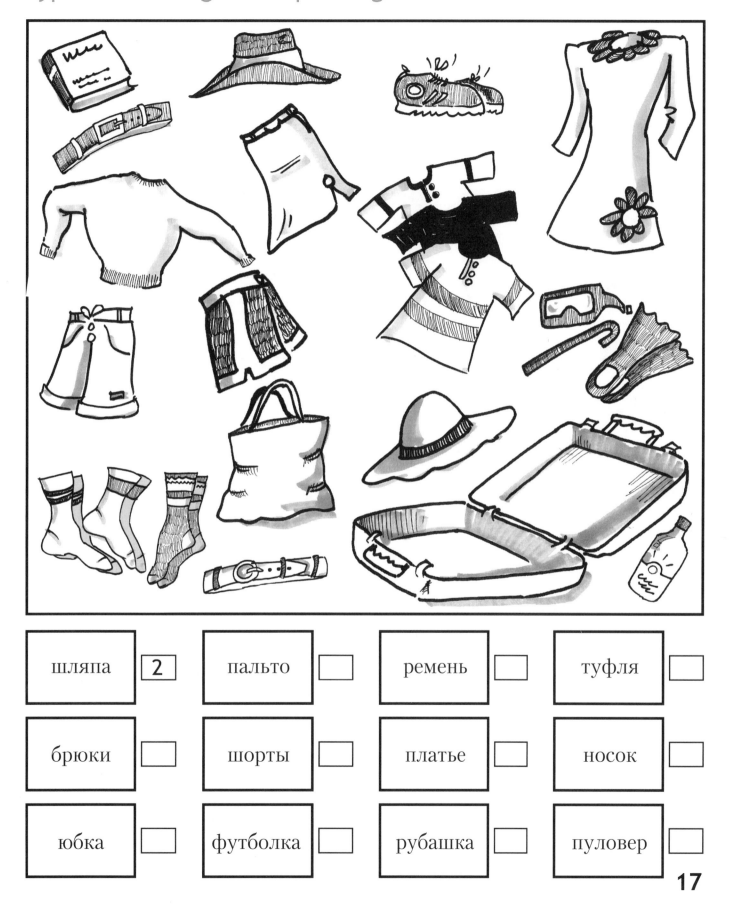

шляпа	2	пальто		ремень		туфля	
брюки		шорты		платье		носок	
юбка		футболка		рубашка		пуловер	

Someone has ripped up the Russian words for clothes.
Can you join the two halves of the words, as the example?

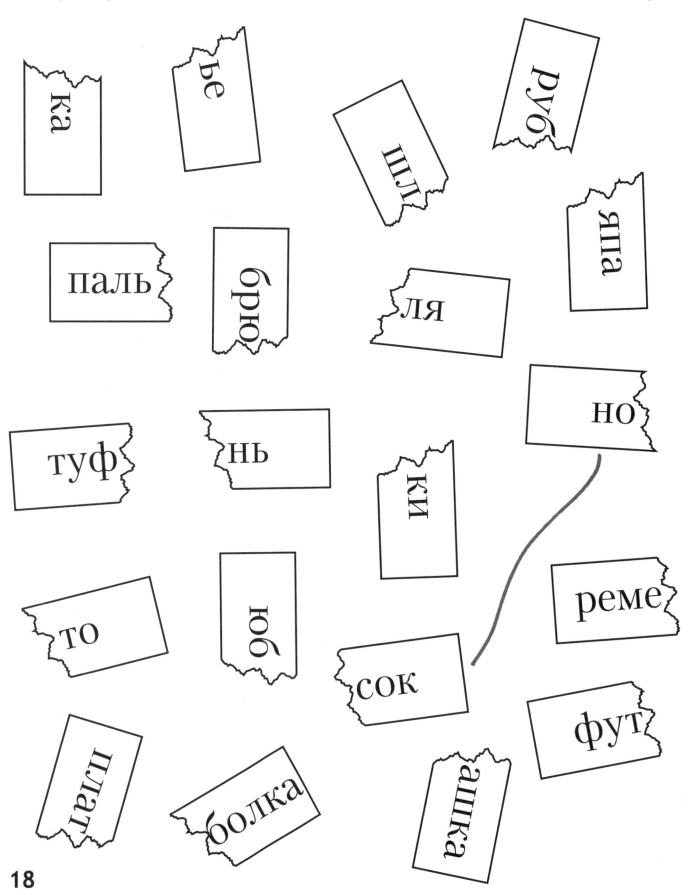

ка

бе

руб

шл

яп

паль

брю

ля

но

туф

нь

ки

рeме

то

юб

сок

фут

плат

болка

ашка

❸ AROUND TOWN

Look at the pictures of things you might find around town.
Tear out the flashcards for this topic.
Follow steps 1 and 2 of the plan in the introduction.

гостиница   *gasteeneetsa*

автобус
aftoboos

дом
dom

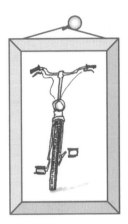

велосипед
vyelaseepyet

машина
masheena

кино
keeno

поезд
poyest

такси   *taksee*

школа   *shkola*

дорога *daroga*

магазин *magazeen*

ресторан
restaran

◎ **M**atch the Russian words to their English equivalents.

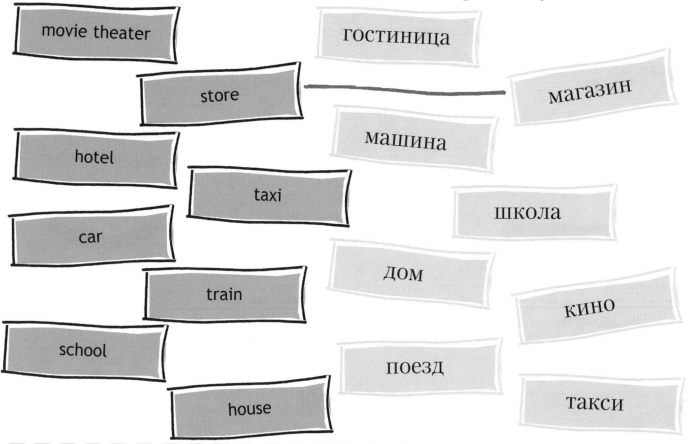

movie theater

гостиница

store ——————— магазин

машина

hotel

taxi

школа

car

дом

train

кино

school

поезд

house

такси

◎ **N**ow list the correct order of the English words to match the Russian word chain, as in the example.

автобус — дом — дорога — велосипед — машина — поезд — такси

bicycle   taxi   house   bus   train   road   car

4

◎ **M**atch the words to the signs.

школа	машина	велосипед	автобус
ресторан	поезд	гостиница	такси

Now choose the Russian word that matches the picture to fill in the English word at the bottom of the page.

такси (c)	машина (f)	дом (s)
дорога (c)	машина (a)	автобус (k)
дом (h)	велосипед (e)	ресторан (u)
дом (b)	велосипед (o)	поезд (w)
школа (o)	дорога (h)	гостиница (s)
гостиница (r)	магазин (g)	кино (l)

English word: (s) ( ) ( ) ( ) ( ) ( )

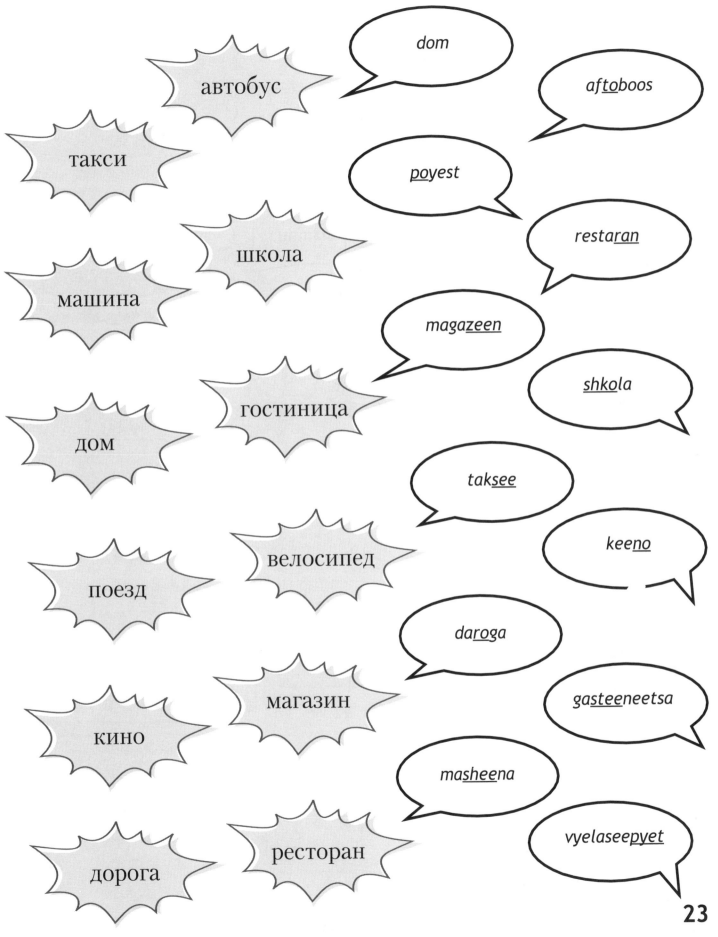

④ COUNTRYSIDE

Look at the pictures of things you might find in the countryside.
Tear out the flashcards for this topic.
Follow steps 1 and 2 of the plan in the introduction.

ХОЛМ
kholm

МОСТ
most

ФЕРМА
ferma

ГОРА
gara

озеро
ozera

дерево
dyereva

цветок
tsvetok

река *reka*

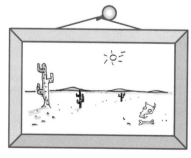

море *morye*

поле *polye*

пустыня
poostinya

лес
lyes

24

Can you match all the countryside words to the pictures.

гора

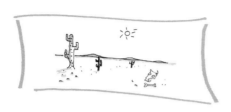 

ферма

море

лес

пустыня

холм

озеро

мост

река

цветок

дерево

поле

Now check (✔) the features you can find in this landscape.

мост	✔	дерево	☐	пустыня	☐	холм	☐
гора	☐	море	☐	поле	☐	лес	☐
озеро	☐	река	☐	цветок	☐	ферма	☐

Match the Russian words and their pronunciation.

гора

река — *reka*

лес — *lyes*

пустыня — *poostinya*

море — *morye*

ферма — *ferma*

мост — *most*

поле — *polye*

gara

See if you can find these words in the word square.
The words can run left to right, or top to bottom.

дерево
ферма
холм
цветок
мост
озеро

е	м	м	н	л	ь	о	я
т	х	о	л	м	ы	ф	л
к	я	с	ш	п	о	е	ь
р	т	т	о	з	е	р	о
е	п	ь	л	о	е	м	н
я	а	т	а	ь	ь	а	л
д	е	р	е	в	о	ш	я
е	ь	ц	в	е	т	о	к

27

Finally, test yourself by joining the Russian words, their pronunciation, and the English meanings, as in the example.

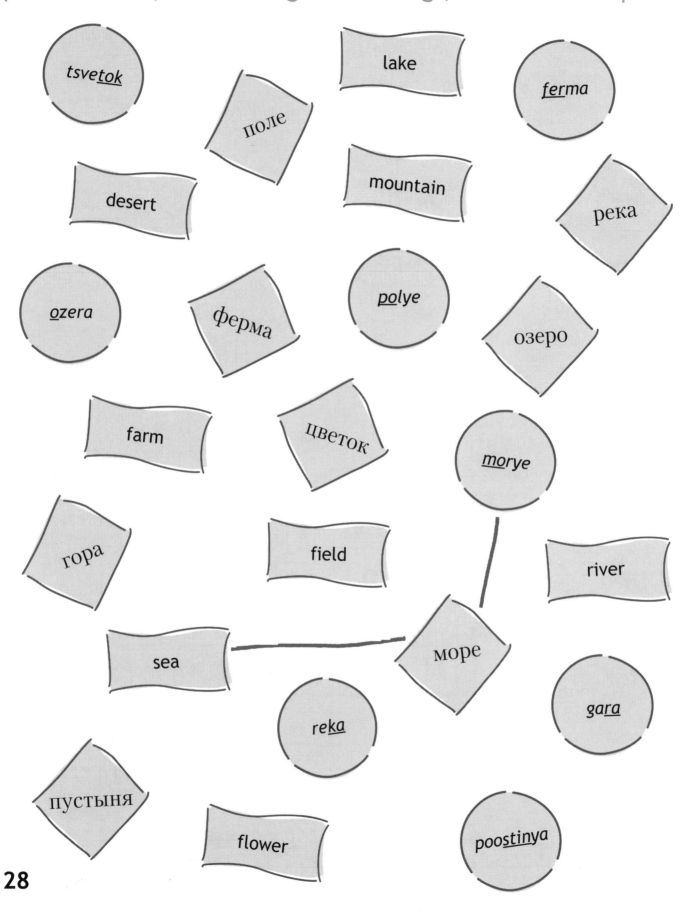

tsvetok

lake

ferma

поле

desert

mountain

река

ozera

ферма

polye

озеро

farm

цветок

morye

гора

field

river

sea

море

gara

reka

пустыня

flower

poostinya

⑤ OPPOSITES

Look at the pictures.
Tear out the flashcards for this topic.
Follow steps 1 and 2 of the plan in the introduction.

грязный
gryazniy

чистый
cheestiy

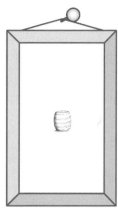

маленький
malyen'keey

большой
bal'shoy

дешёвый
deshoviy

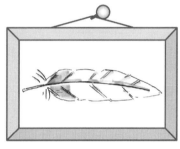

лёгкий *lyokhkeey*

медленный *myedlenniy*

дорогой *daragoy*

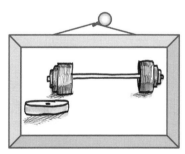

тяжёлый *teezholiy*

быстрый *bistriy*

старый *stariy*

новый *noviy*

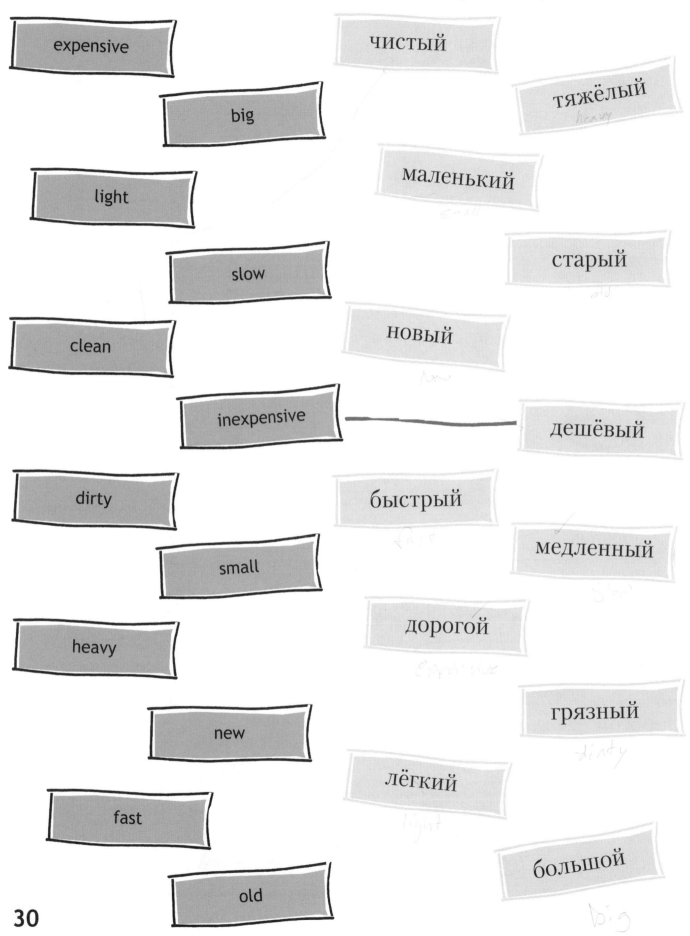

expensive

чистый

тяжёлый
heavy

big

маленький
small

light

старый
old

slow

новый
new

clean

inexpensive —————— дешёвый

dirty

быстрый
fast

медленный
slow

small

дорогой
expensive

heavy

грязный
dirty

new

лёгкий
light

fast

большой
big

30

old

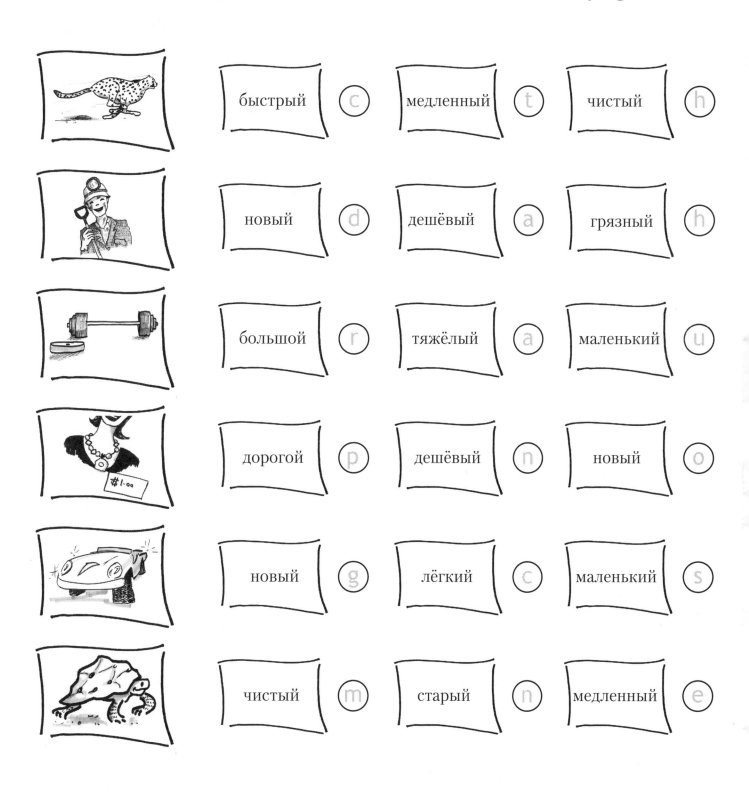

Now choose the Russian word that matches the picture to fill in the English word at the bottom of the page.

быстрый (c)	медленный (t)	чистый (h)
новый (d)	дешёвый (a)	грязный (h)
большой (r)	тяжёлый (a)	маленький (u)
дорогой (p)	дешёвый (n)	новый (o)
новый (g)	лёгкий (c)	маленький (s)
чистый (m)	старый (n)	медленный (e)

E nglish word: ○ ○ ○ ○ ○ ○

Find the odd one out in these groups of words.

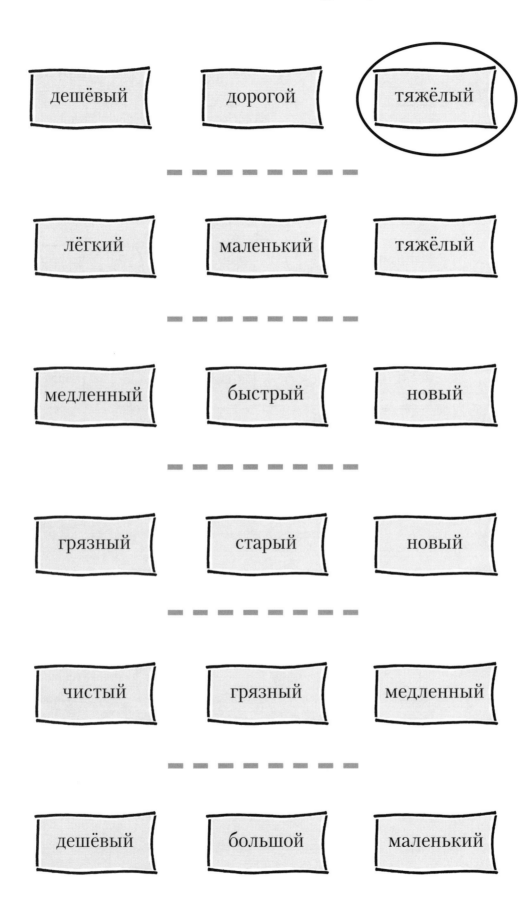

дешёвый	дорогой	(тяжёлый)
лёгкий	маленький	тяжёлый
медленный	быстрый	новый
грязный	старый	новый
чистый	грязный	медленный
дешёвый	большой	маленький

Finally, join the English words to their Russian opposites, as in the example.

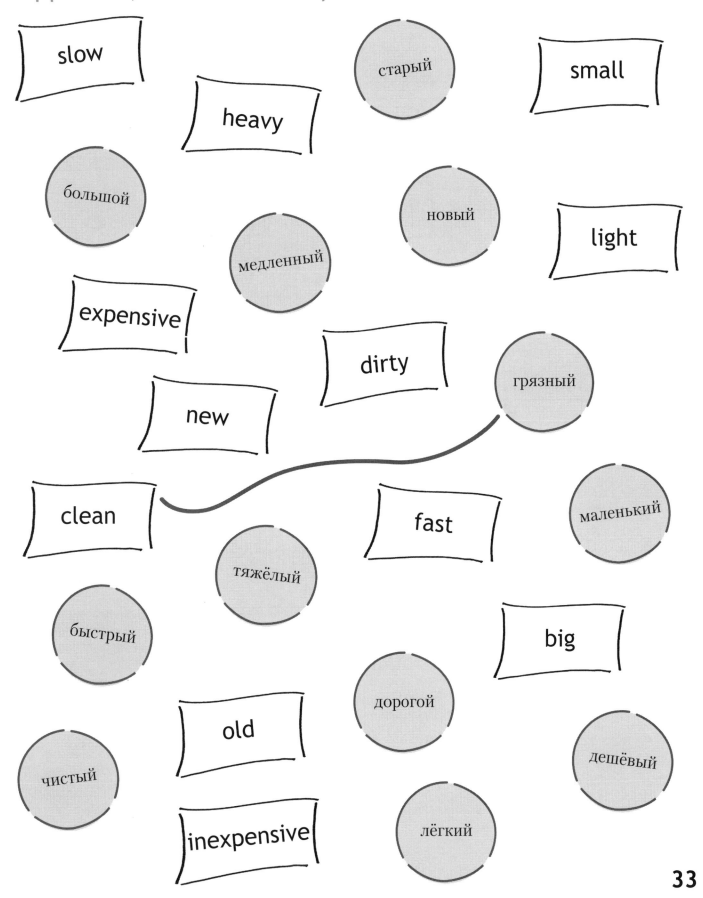

slow

heavy

старый

small

большой

новый

light

медленный

expensive

dirty

грязный

new

clean

fast

маленький

тяжёлый

быстрый

big

дорогой

old

дешёвый

чистый

inexpensive

лёгкий

6 ANIMALS

Look at the pictures.
Tear out the flashcards for this topic.
Follow steps 1 and 2 of the plan in the introduction.

утка *ootka*

слон
slon

кошка
koshka

собака
sabaka

кролик
kroleek

обезьяна
abes'yana

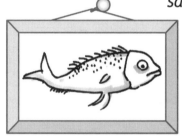

рыба *riba*

овца *avtsa*

мышь *mish'*

корова *karova*

лошадь
loshat'

лев
lev

34

Match the animals to their associated pictures, as in the example.

кролик

лошадь

обезьяна

кошка

овца

мышь

собака

лев

корова

рыба

35

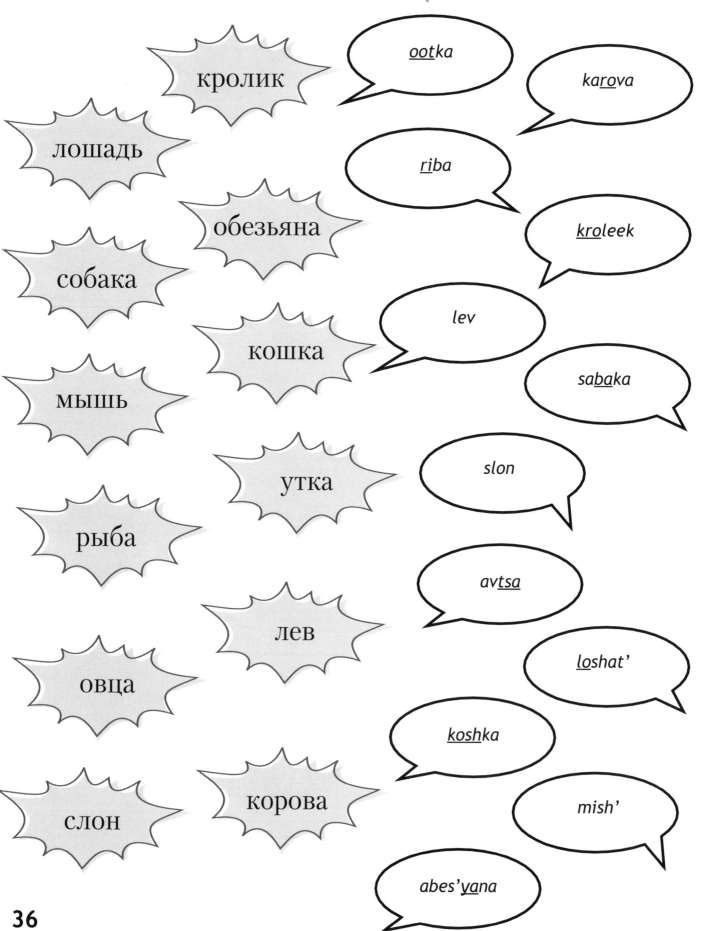

Check (✔) the animal words you can find in the word pile.

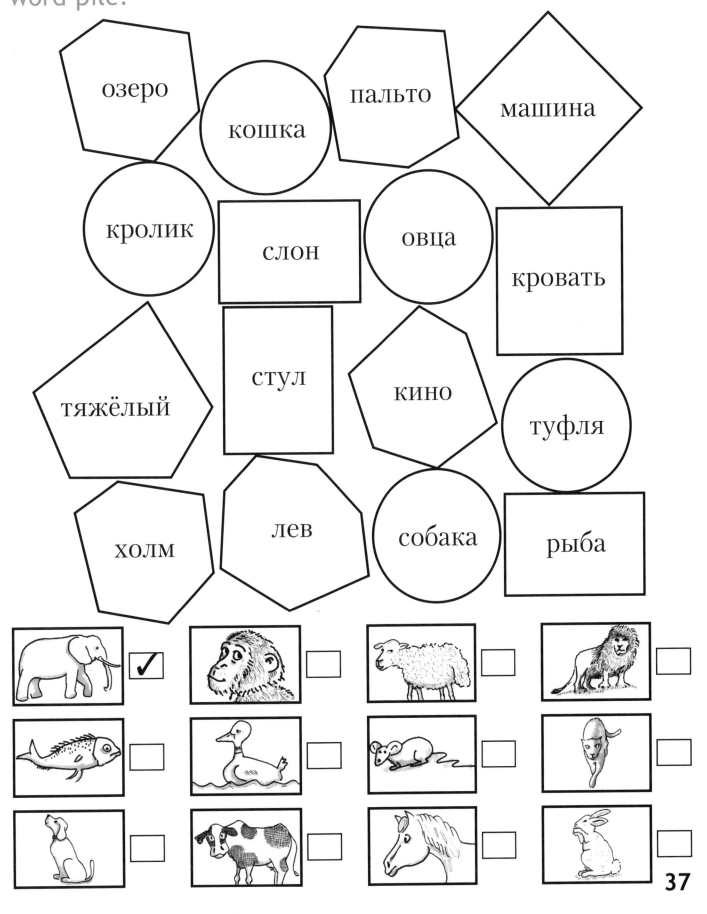

озеро

кошка

пальто

машина

кролик

слон

овца

кровать

тяжёлый

стул

кино

туфля

холм

лев

собака

рыба

Join the Russian animals to their English equivalents.

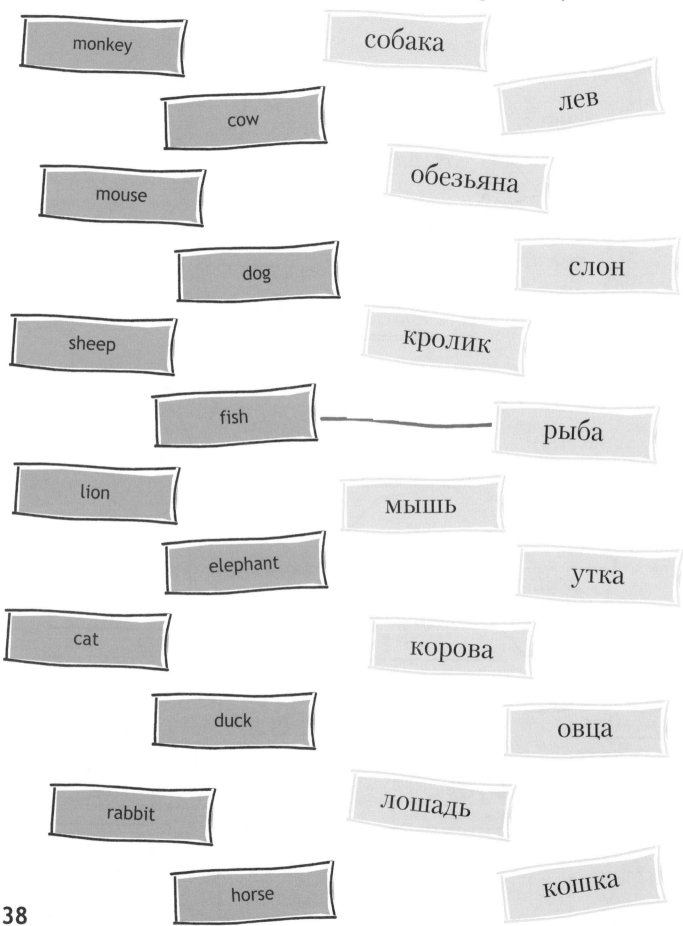

monkey

собака

лев

cow

обезьяна

mouse

слон

dog

кролик

sheep

fish ——— рыба

lion

мышь

elephant

утка

cat

корова

duck

овца

rabbit

лошадь

horse

кошка

⑦ PARTS OF THE BODY

Look at the pictures of parts of the body.
Tear out the flashcards for this topic.
Follow steps 1 and 2 of the plan in the introduction.

палец
palets

голова
galava

рука
rooka

глаз *glas*

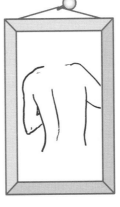

спина
speena

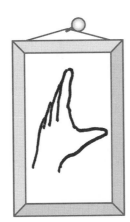

рука
rooka

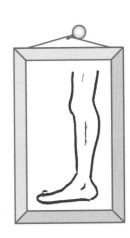

нога
naga

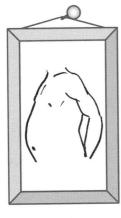

живот
zheevot

волосы *volasi*

ухо
ookha

нос
nos

рот
rot

39

Someone has ripped up the Russian words for parts of the body. Can you join the two halves of the word again?

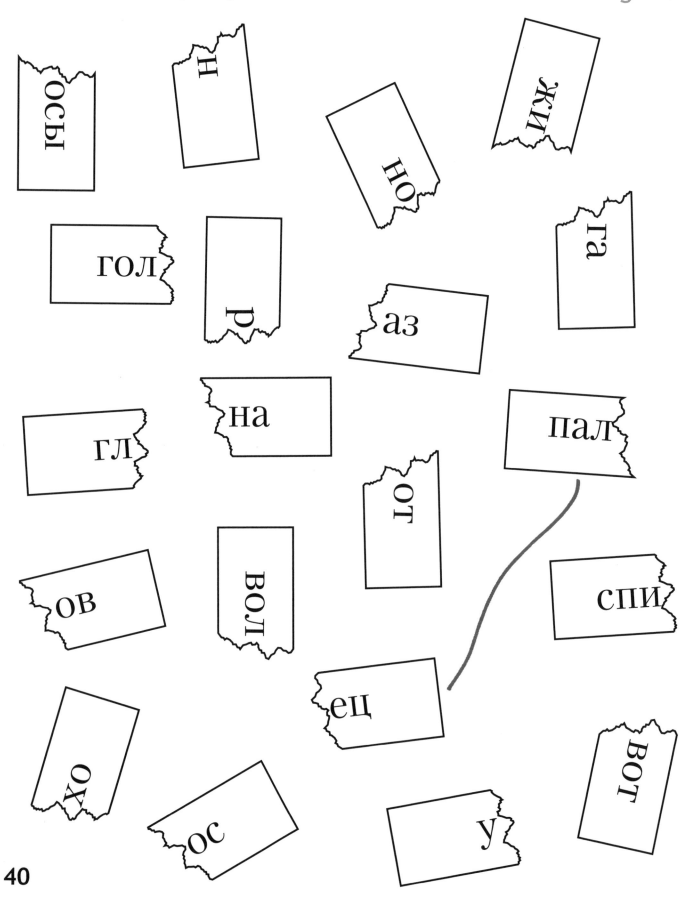

осы

н

но

жи

гол

р

га

аз

на

пал

гл

от

ов

вол

спи

ец

ох

вот

ос

у

◎ **S**ee if you can find and circle six parts of the body in the word square, then draw them in the boxes below.

The words can run left to right, or top to bottom:

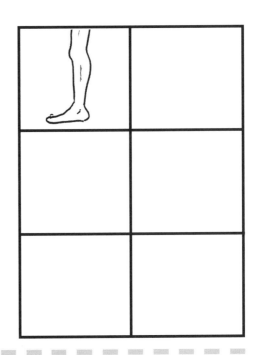

◎ **N**ow match the Russian to the pronunciation.

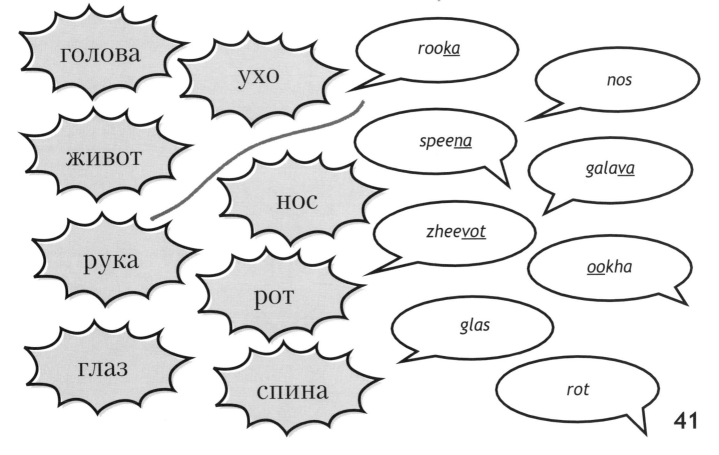

голова   ухо   *rooka*   *nos*

живот   нос   *speena*   *galava*

рука   рот   *zheevot*   *ookha*

глаз   спина   *glas*   *rot*

41

Label the body with the correct number, and write the pronunciation next to the words.

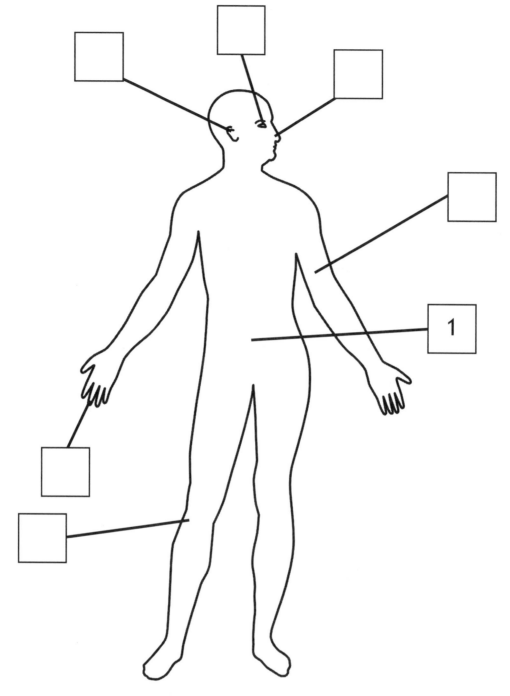

1 живот _zheevot_

2 рука

3 нос

4 ухо

5 нога

6 глаз

7 палец

Finally, match the Russian words, their pronunciation, and the English meanings, as in the example.

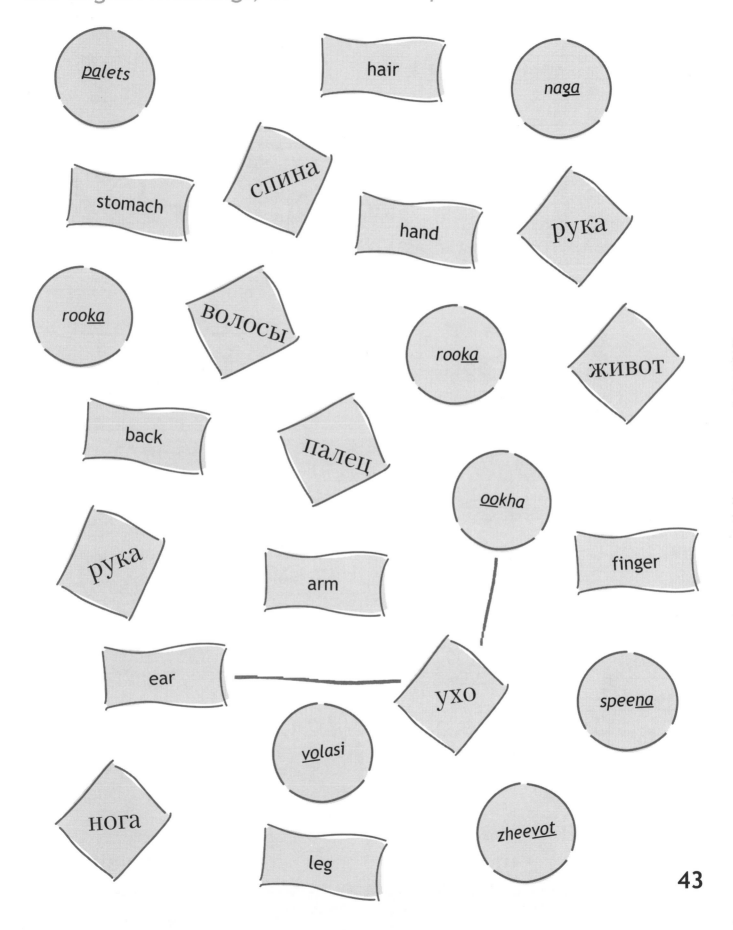

palets

hair

naga

спина

stomach

hand

рука

rooka

волосы

rooka

живот

back

палец

ookha

рука

arm

finger

ear

ухо

speena

volasi

нога

zheevot

leg

8 USEFUL EXPRESSIONS

Look at the pictures.
Tear out the flashcards for this topic.
Follow steps 1 and 2 of the plan in the introduction.

где? *gdye*

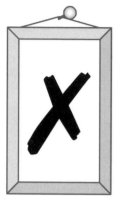

нет
nyet

да
da

здравствуйте
zdrastvooytye

до свидания
da sveedaneeya

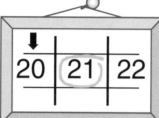

вчера
fchyera

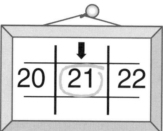

сегодня
sevodnya

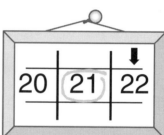

завтра
zaftra

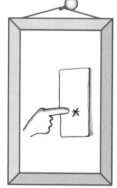

здесь
zdyes'

там *tam*

сейчас *seechas*

сколько стоит?
skol'ka stoeet

извините!
eezveeneetye

отлично!
atleechna

пожалуйста
pazhalsta

спасибо
spaseeba

44

Match the Russian words to their English equivalents.

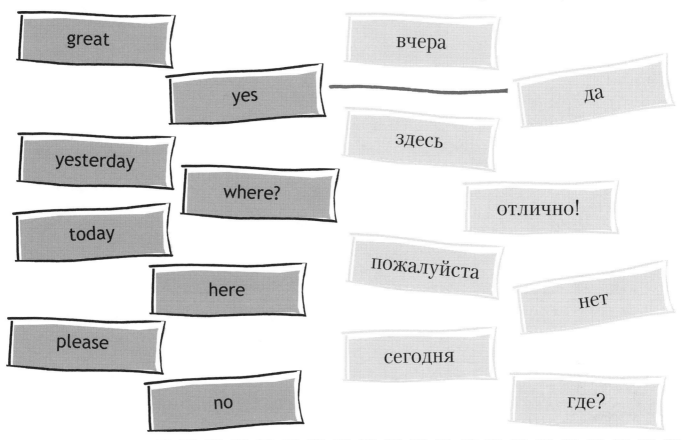

Now match the Russian to the pronunciation.

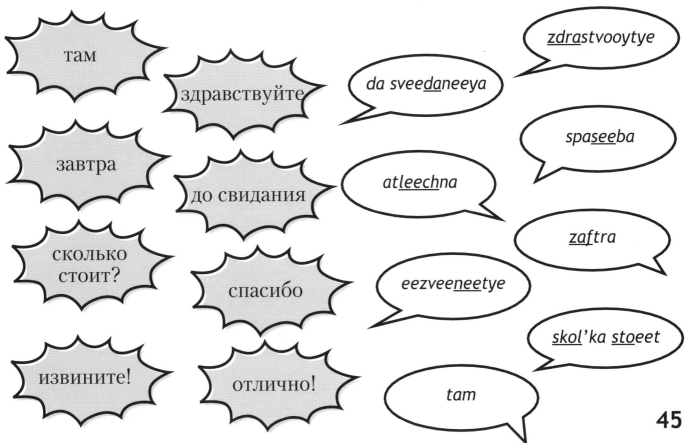

45

Choose the Russian word that matches the picture to fill in the English word at the bottom of the page.

здесь (p)	нет (c)	да (t)
спасибо (j)	извините! (a)	пожалуйста (l)
да (m)	нет (e)	сегодня (i)
там (b)	здравствуйте (a)	пожалуйста (x)
где? (s)	сегодня (h)	*fchyera* (t)
здравствуйте (b)	нет (y)	да (e)

English word: (p) ( ) ( ) ( ) ( ) ( )

46

What are these people saying? Write the correct number in each speech bubble, as in the example.

1. здравствуйте   2. пожалуйста   3. да   4. нет

5. здесь   6. извините!   7. где?   8. сколько стоит?

Finally, match the Russian words, their pronunciation, and the English meanings, as in the example.

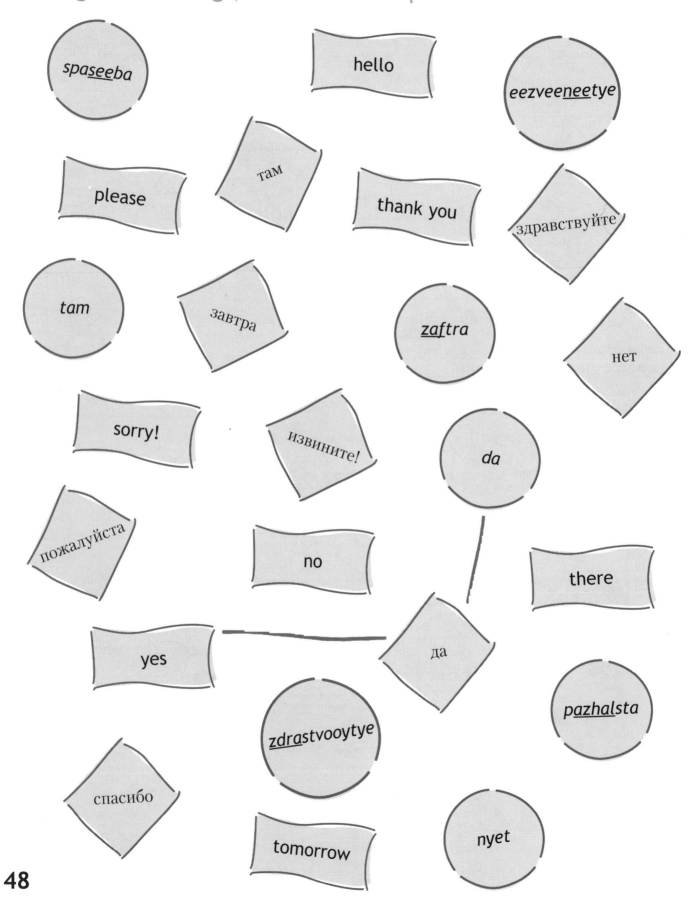

spa<u>see</u>ba

hello

eezvee<u>nee</u>tye

please

там

thank you

здравствуйте

tam

завтра

<u>za</u>ftra

нет

sorry!

извините!

da

пожалуйста

no

there

yes

да

pa<u>zhal</u>sta

<u>zdra</u>stvooytye

спасибо

tomorrow

nyet

48

● ROUND-UP

This section is designed to review all the 100 words you have met in the different topics. It is a good idea to test yourself with your flashcards before trying this section.

◎ These ten objects are hidden in the picture. Can you find and circle them?

дверь   цветок   кровать   пальто   шляпа

велосипед   стул   собака   рыба   носок

See if you can remember all these words.

сегодня

автобус

быстрый

нос

пустыня

да

шкаф

лев

платье

дешёвый

река

нога

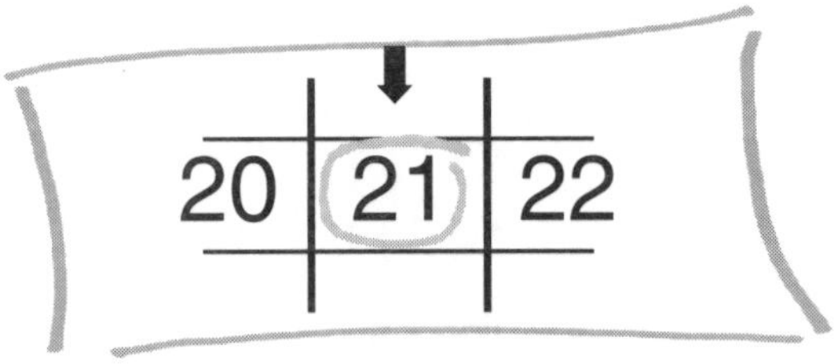

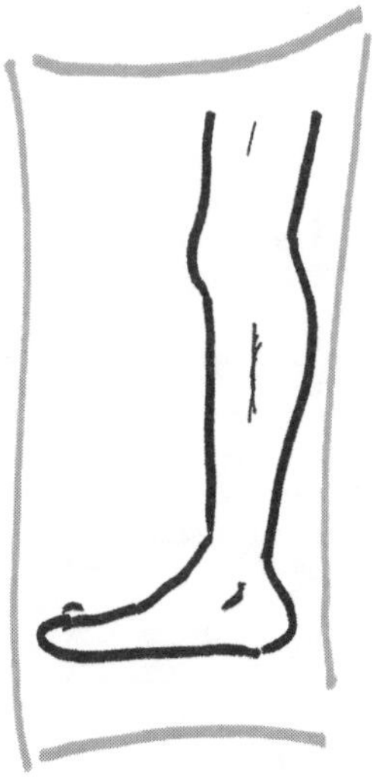

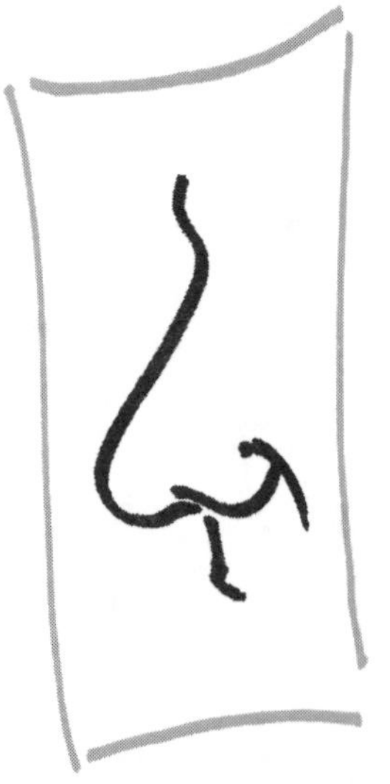

Find the odd one out in these groups of words and say why.

| собака | корова | (стол) | обезьяна |

Because it isn't an animal.

| машина | автобус | поезд | телефон |

| ферма | пальто | рубашка | юбка |

| море | озеро | река | дерево |

| дорогой | грязный | чистый | кино |

| кролик | кошка | рыба | лев |

| рука | софа | голова | живот |

| пожалуйста | вчера | завтра | сегодня |

| плита | кровать | шкаф | холодильник |

Look at the objects below for 30 seconds.

Cover the picture and try to remember all the objects.
Circle the Russian words for those you remember.

цветок　　　туфля　　　спасибо　　　дверь

кошка　　　здесь　　　пальто　　　поезд
　　　нет

ремень　　гора　　машина　　стул　　лошадь

носок　　футболка　　глаз　　кровать

шорты　　такси　　телевизор　　обезьяна

Now match the Russian words, their pronunciation, and the English meanings, as in the example.

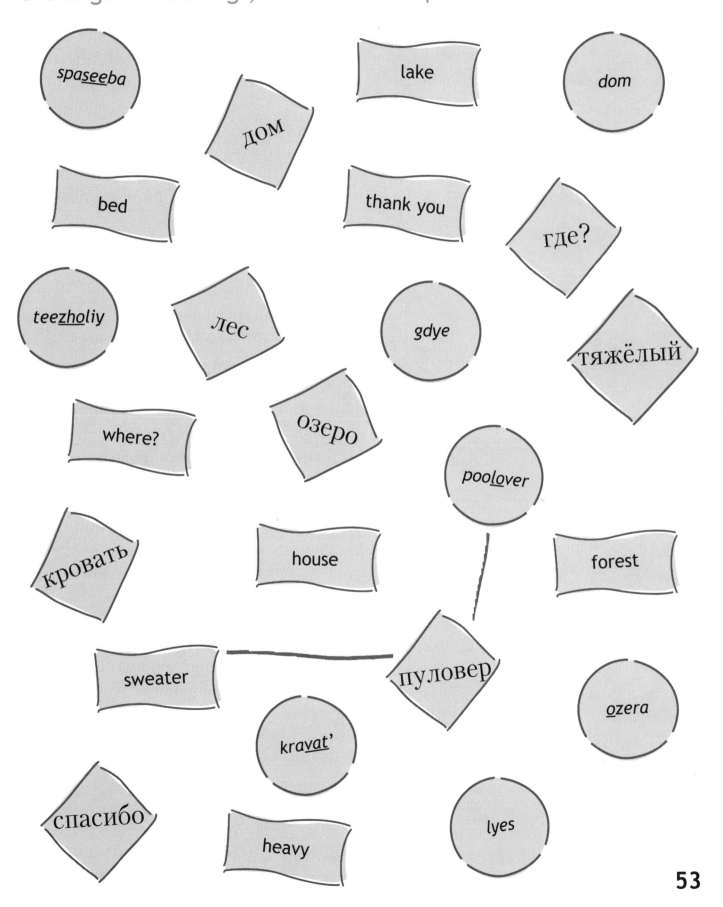

spaseeba

lake

dom

ДОМ

bed

thank you

где?

teezholiy

лес

gdye

тяжёлый

where?

озеро

poolover

кровать

house

forest

sweater

пуловер

ozera

спасибо

kravat'

lyes

heavy

53

софа	w	такси	g	ухо	t
пальто	o	грязный	a	мост	e
да	m	сколько стоит?	l	сегодня	i
корова	b	окно	l	ресторан	h
где?	e	рот	a	собака	d
глаз	o	стол	p	здравствуйте	v
холм	n	нет	y	автобус	r
кролик	n	дорога	e	плита	s

English phrase: w ◯ ◯ ◯   ◯ ◯ ◯ ◯ !

Look at the two pictures and check (✔) the objects that are different in Picture B.

Picture A

шорты	
футболка	
дверь	
кошка	
стул	
рыба	
носок	
собака	

Picture B

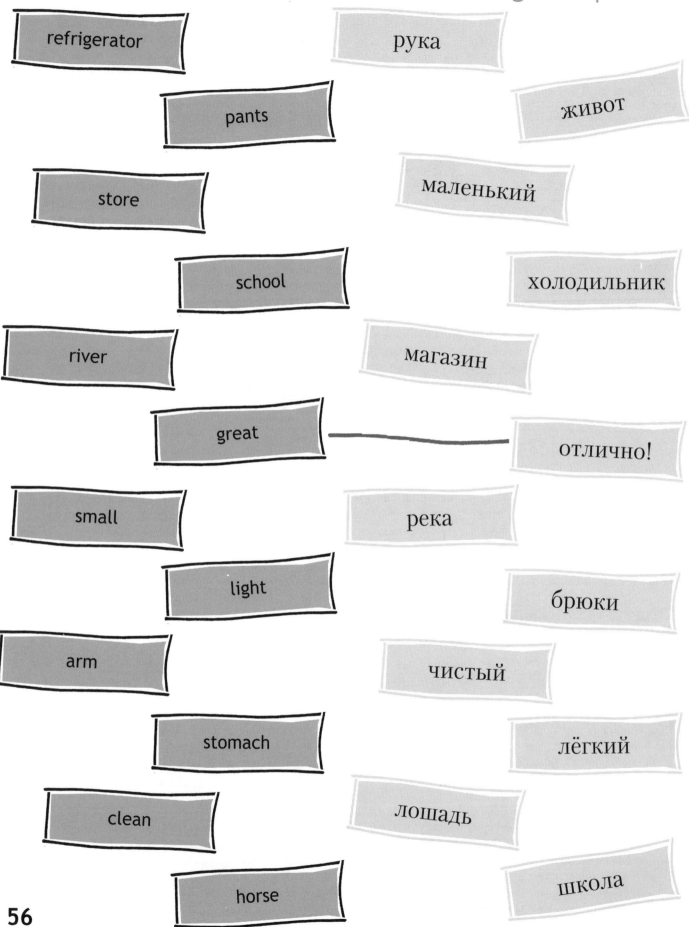

refrigerator

рука

pants

живот

store

маленький

school

холодильник

river

магазин

great ———————— отлично!

small

река

light

брюки

arm

чистый

stomach

лёгкий

clean

лошадь

horse

школа

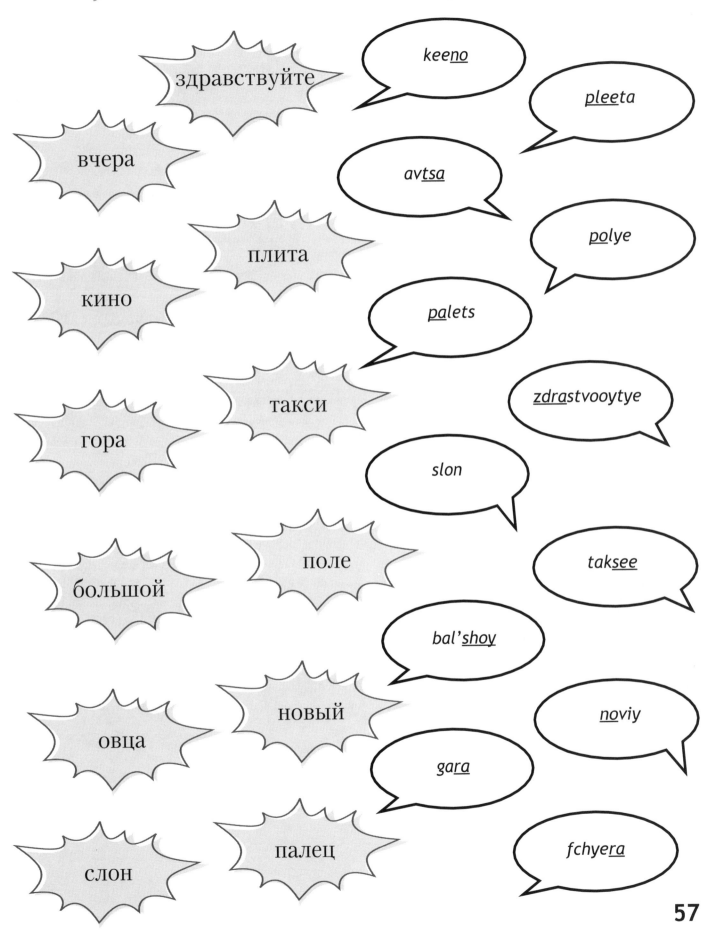

57

◎ Snake game.

- You will need a die and counter(s). You can challenge yourself to reach the finish or play with someone else. You have to throw the exact number to finish.

- Throw the die and move forward that number of spaces. When you land on a word you must pronounce it and say what it means in English. If you can't, you have to go back to the square you came from.

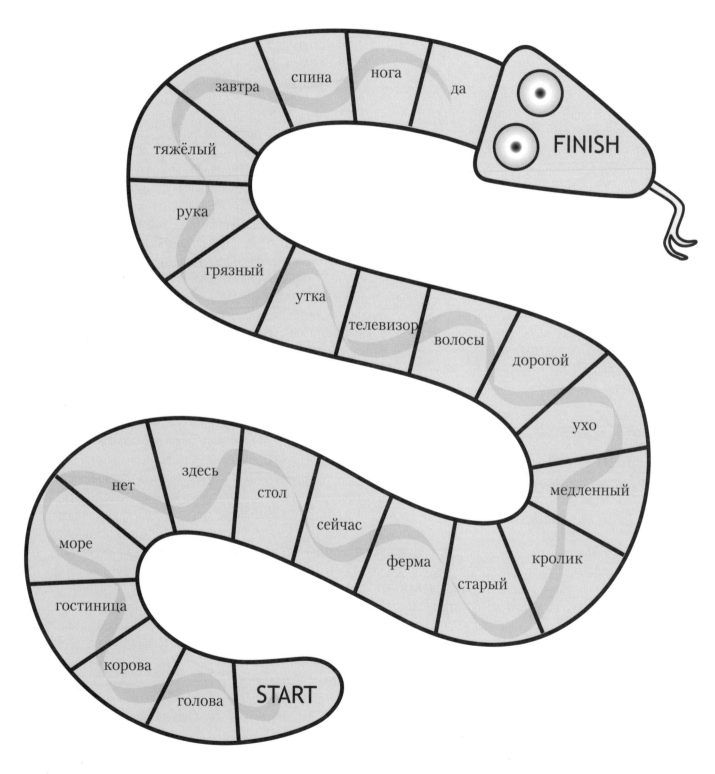

Answers

① AROUND THE HOME

Page 10 (top)

See page 9 for correct picture.

Page 10 (bottom)

door	дверь
cupboard	шкаф
stove	плита
bed	кровать
table	стол
chair	стул
refrigerator	холодильник
computer	компьютер

Page 11 (top)

стол	*stol*
шкаф	*shkaf*
компьютер	*kampyooter*
кровать	*kravat'*
окно	*akno*
телефон	*telefon*
телевизор	*televeezar*
стул	*stool*

Page 11 (bottom)

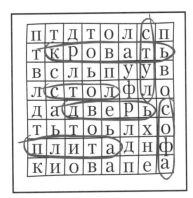

Page 12

Page 13

English word: window

② CLOTHES

Page 15 (top)

платье	*plat'e*
шорты	*shorti*
туфля	*tooflya*
ремень	*remyen'*
рубашка	*roobashka*
футболка	*footbolka*
шляпа	*shlyapa*
носок	*nasok*

Page 15 (bottom)

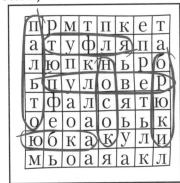

Page 16

hat	шляпа	*shlyapa*
shoe	туфля	*tooflya*
sock	носок	*nasok*
shorts	шорты	*shorti*
T-shirt	футболка	*footbolka*
belt	ремень	*remyen'*
coat	пальто	*pal'to*
pants/trousers	брюки	*bryookee*

Page 17

шляпа (hat)	2
пальто (coat)	0
ремень (belt)	2
туфля (shoe)	2 (1 pair)
брюки (pants)	0
шорты (shorts)	2
платье (dress)	1
носок (sock)	6 (3 pairs)
юбка (skirt)	1
футболка (t-shirt)	3
рубашка (shirt)	0
пуловер (sweater)	1

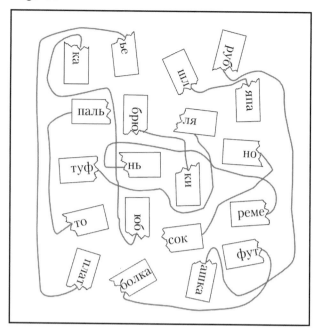

③ AROUND TOWN

Page 20 (top)

movie theater	кино
store	магазин
hotel	гостиница
taxi	такси
car	машина
train	поезд
school	школа
house	дом

Page 20 (bottom)

bicycle	4
taxi	7
house	2
train	6
bus	1
road	3
car	5

Page 21

школа   такси   автобус

машина   поезд   ресторан

гостиница   велосипед

Page 22

English word: school

Page 23

автобус	*aftoboos*
такси	*taksee*
школа	*shkola*
машина	*masheena*
гостиница	*gasteeneets*
дом	*dom*
велосипед	*vyelaseepyet*
поезд	*poyest*
магазин	*magazeen*
кино	*keeno*
ресторан	*restaran*
дорога	*daroga*

④ COUNTRYSIDE

Page 25

See page 24 for correct picture.

Page 26

мост	✔	поле	✔
дерево	✔	лес	✔
пустыня	✘	озеро	✘
холм	✘	река	✔
гора	✔	цветок	✔
море	✘	ферма	✔

Page 27 (top)

гора	*gara*
река	*reka*
лес	*lyes*
пустыня	*poostinya*
море	*morye*
ферма	*ferma*
мост	*most*
поле	*polye*

Page 27 (bottom)

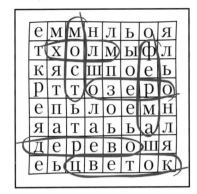

Page 28

sea	море	*morye*
lake	озеро	*ozera*
desert	пустыня	*poostinya*
farm	ферма	*ferma*
flower	цветок	*tsvetok*
mountain	гора	*gara*
river	река	*reka*
field	поле	*polye*

❺ OPPOSITES

Page 30

expensive	дорогой
big	большой
light	лёгкий
slow	медленный
clean	чистый
inexpensive	дешёвый
dirty	грязный
small	маленький
heavy	тяжёлый
new	новый
fast	быстрый
old	старый

Page 31

English word: change

Page 32

Odd one outs are those which are not opposites:

тяжёлый
маленький
новый
грязный
медленный
дешёвый

Page 33

old	новый
big	маленький
new	старый
slow	быстрый
dirty	чистый
small	большой
heavy	лёгкий
clean	грязный
light	тяжёлый
expensive	дешёвый
inexpensive	дорогой

❻ ANIMALS

Page 35

корова   кролик   рыба   лев

овца   собака   обезьяна

лошадь   мышь   кошка

Page 36

кролик	*kroleek*
лошадь	*loshat'*
обезьяна	*abes'yana*
собака	*sabaka*
кошка	*koshka*
мышь	*mish'*
утка	*ootka*
рыба	*riba*
лев	*lev*
овца	*avtsa*
корова	*karova*
слон	*slon*

Page 37

elephant	✔	mouse	✘
monkey	✘	cat	✔
sheep	✔	dog	✘
lion	✔	cow	✔
fish	✔	horse	✘
duck	✘	rabbit	✔

Page 38

monkey	обезьяна
cow	корова
mouse	мышь
dog	собака
sheep	овца
fish	рыба
lion	лев
elephant	слон
cat	кошка
duck	утка
rabbit	кролик
horse	лошадь

❼ PARTS OF THE BODY

Page 40

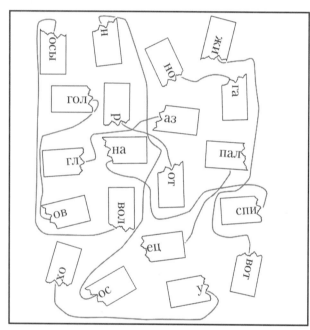

Page 41 (top)

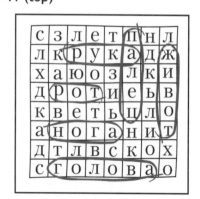

You should have also drawn pictures of:

leg; mouth; hand/arm; finger; stomach; head

Page 41 (bottom)

голова	*galava*
ухо	*ookha*
живот	*zheevot*
нос	*nos*
рука	*rooka*
рот	*rot*
глаз	*glas*
спина	*speena*

Page 42

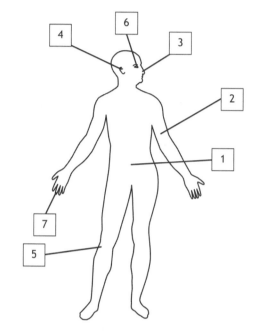

1.	живот	*zheevot*
2.	рука	*rooka*
3.	нос	*nos*
4.	ухо	*ookha*
5.	нога	*naga*
6.	глаз	*glas*
7.	палец	*palets*

Page 43

ear	ухо	*ookha*
hair	волосы	*volasi*
hand	рука	*rooka*
stomach	живот	*zheevot*
arm	рука	*rooka*
back	спина	*speena*
finger	палец	*palets*
leg	нога	*naga*

⑧ USEFUL EXPRESSIONS

Page 45 (top)

great!	отлично!
yes	да
yesterday	вчера
where?	где?
today	сегодня
here	здесь
please	пожалуйста
no	нет

Page 45 (bottom)

там	*tam*
здравствуйте	*zdrastvooytye*
завтра	*zaftra*
до свидания	*da sveedaneeya*
сколько стоит?	*skol'ka stoeet*
спасибо	*spaseeba*
извините!	*eezveeneetye*
отлично!	*atleechna*

Page 46

English word: please

Page 47

Page 48

yes	да	da
hello	здравствуйте	zdrastvooytye
no	нет	nyet
sorry!	извините!	eezveeneetye
please	пожалуйста	pazhalsta
there	там	tam
thank you	спасибо	spaseeba
tomorrow	завтра	zaftra

● ROUND-UP

Page 49

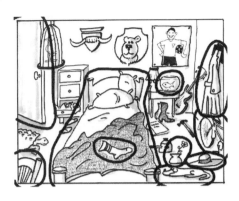

Page 50

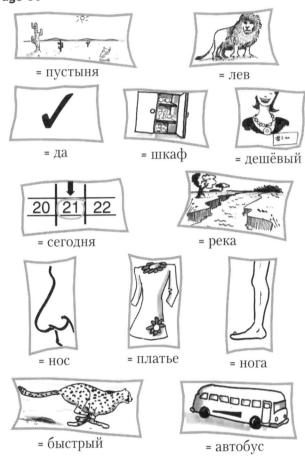

= пустыня

= лев

= да

= шкаф

= дешёвый

= сегодня

= река

= нос

= платье

= нога

= быстрый

= автобус

Page 51

стол (Because it isn't an animal.)

телефон (Because it isn't a means of transportation.)

ферма (Because it isn't an item of clothing.)

дерево (Because it isn't connected with water.)

кино (Because it isn't a descriptive word.)

рыба (Because it lives in water/doesn't have legs.)

софа (Because it isn't a part of the body.)

пожалуйста (Because it isn't an expression of time.)

кровать (Because you wouldn't find it in the kitchen.)

Page 52

Words that appear in the picture:

футболка
машина
цветок
туфля
поезд
обезьяна
телевизор
стул
ремень
шорты

Page 53

sweater	пуловер	*poolover*
lake	озеро	*ozera*
thank you	спасибо	*spaseebaou*
bed	кровать	*kravat'*
house	дом	*dom*
forest	лес	*lyes*
where?	где?	*gdye*
heavy	тяжёлый	*teezholiy*

Page 54

English phrase: well done!

Page 55

шорты	✔ (shade)
футболка	✗
дверь	✔ (handle)
кошка	✗
стул	✔ (back)
рыба	✔ (direction)
носок	✔ (pattern)
собака	✗

Page 56

refrigerator	холодильник
pants	брюки
store	магазин
school	школа
river	река
great!	отлично!
small	маленький
light	лёгкий
arm	рука
stomach	живот
clean	чистый
horse	лошадь

Page 57

здравствуйте	*zdrastvooytye*
вчера	*fchyera*
плита	*pleeta*
кино	*keeno*
такси	*taksee*
гора	*gara*
поле	*polye*
большой	*bal'shoy*
новый	*noviy*
овца	*avtsa*
палец	*palets*
слон	*slon*

Page 58

Here are the English equivalents of the words, in order from START to FINISH:

head	*galava*	ear	*ookha*
cow	*karova*	expensive	*daragoy*
hotel	*gasteeneetsa*	hair	*volasi*
sea	*morye*	television	*televeezar*
no	*nyet*	duck	*ootka*
here	*zdyes'*	dirty	*gryazniy*
table	*stol*	hand	*rooka*
now	*seechas*	heavy	*teezholiy*
farm	*ferma*	tomorrow	*zaftra*
old	*stariy*	back	*speena*
rabbit	*kroleek*	leg	*naga*
slow	*myedlenniy*	yes	*da*

64

озеро

ozera

лес

lyes

холм

kholm

море

morye

гора

gara

дерево

dyereva

пустыня

poostinya

цветок

tsvetok

мост

most

река

reka

ферма

ferma

поле

polye

forest	lake
sea	hill
tree	mountain
flower	desert
river	bridge
field	farm

озеро *ozera*	**лес** *lyes*
холм *kholm*	**море** *morye*
гора *gara*	**дерево** *dyereva*
пустыня *poostinya*	**цветок** *tsvetok*
мост *most*	**река** *reka*
ферма *ferma*	**поле** *polye*

forest	lake
sea	hill
tree	mountain
flower	desert
river	bridge
field	farm

тяжёлый *teezholiy*	лёгкий *lyokhkeey*
большой *bal'shoy*	маленький *malyen'keey*
старый *stariy*	новый *noviy*
быстрый *bistriy*	медленный *myedlenniy*
чистый *cheestiy*	грязный *gryazniy*
дешёвый *deshoviy*	дорогой *daragoy*

light	heavy
small	big
new	old
slow	fast
dirty	clean
expensive	cheap

утка

ootka

кошка

koshka

мышь

mish'

корова

karova

кролик

kroleek

собака

sabaka

лошадь

loshat'

обезьяна

abes'yana

лев

lev

рыба

riba

слон

slon

овца

avtsa

cat

duck

cow

mouse

dog

rabbit

monkey

horse

fish

lion

sheep

elephant

рука

rooka

палец

palets

голова

galava

рот

rot

ухо

ookha

нога

naga

рука

rooka

живот

zheevot

глаз

glas

волосы

volasi

нос

nos

спина

speena

finger	arm
mouth	head
leg	ear
stomach	hand
hair	eye
back	nose

8

пожалуйста
pazhalsta

спасибо
spaseeba

да
da

нет
nyet

здравствуйте
zdrastvooytye

до свидания
]da sveedaneeya

вчера
fchyera

сегодня
sevodnya

завтра
zaftra

где?
gdye

здесь
zdyes'

там
tam

извините!
eezveeneetye

сколько стоит?
skol'ka stoeet

отлично!
atleechna

сейча
seechas

thank you	please
no	yes
goodbye	hello
today	yesterday
where?	tomorrow
there	here
how much?	sorry!
now	great!